Under Comm in a Day

Stefan Bernstein

TAKE THAT LTD.

Take That Ltd.
P.O.Box 200
Harrogate
HG1 2YR
sales@takethat.co.uk
Fax: +44-1423-526035

You should take independent financial advice before acting on material contained in this book.

Printed and bound in Great Britain.

ISBN 1-873668-46-5

Contents

Author's Preface

When we first produced *Understand Derivatives In a Day*, we knew there was a demand for such clear and relatively simple guides to relatively complicated financial subjects. However, we have been surprised and delighted by the demand. Not only have I seen the book in regular use throughout the various dealing rooms of the world, but it can also be found in the living rooms of those who are simply interested in the subject, are striving to improve their portfolios, or even make a living from trading derivatives.

Readers have included not only professionals and domestic investors, but also students, both in the UK and throughout the world, and the recent translation of the book into east European and Asian languages ensures further, wider distribution.

However, we give the same warning to readers of this book who will be aware of the fantastic gains, and, possibly, greater losses, that can be made in trading in commodities. We have included sections on trading strategies and the reader will not fail to see the emphasis on the risks themselves, and the management of those inherent risks.

As usual, I would like to thank the many professionals and private individuals who have given freely of their time in helping to complete this book. As well as my family and friends who have, once again, given generous support in the many long nights and intense weekends of research which have gone into it's production.

Finally, the greatest thanks on this occasion must go to Alex Kiam, whose understanding of risk in investment has greatly enhanced my own.

Introduction

Call it commodities trading or dealing in Futures, it still has a ring of mystery and excitement about it. Some of this comes as a result of many of the trades being made in both "intangibles" such as stock indices, and actual physical commodities such as sugar. Or it may simply be because so few people really understand what happens in the various dealing rooms and trading pits where chaos seems to reign, and those with the loudest voices and wildest gesticulations seem to come out on top.

It is precisely because of that mystery that this book has been written. It sets out to tell the reader precisely what trading in commodities involves, where it is done, how it is done, and by whom. It goes on further to look at the history of trading, the various systems available, examining fundamental and technical analysis and looking at ways in which the inevitable losses involved might be stemmed.

Finally, in helping the reader to develop his or her own particular trading strategy, there is a consideration of how an individual's own psychological make-up will affect their likelihood of success.

The famous trader, Jack Schwager, has told how on one day, in the 1990s, due simply to one unfortunate word in the U.S. Defence Secretary's speech, he managed to lose $9.5 million in 10 seconds. At the same time, there are numerous reports of traders who began in commodities with a relatively modest sum, and who now have fortunes exceeding $100 million.

That is certainly reason enough to be interested in the chapters which follow, because the stakes are inevitably so very high, and the results, either way, so dramatic.

How To Use This Book

Whilst we recognise that many will return to specific chapters in this book in order to address particular matters, it is essential that in the first instance, you read the whole book. This is because all the information is given in a particular context and with a view to helping you create a particular approach to the matter. To read the chapters on trading strategies, without understanding the basics of fundamental or technical analysis, and without putting them in the context of your own psychological profile, would certainly be a mistake.

Additionally, it would be wise to read one or two of the more general works in the bibliography so as to put this text into some sort of wider context. Finally, once you have decided which type of trading strategy you will take, you need to read as much as you can which is specific to that strategy.

Remember, there is a well used warning that "investments can go down as well as up". The beauty of commodities, is that you can make money either way! Good Luck.

By the same author...
Understand Derivatives in a Day

... and in the same series...
Understand Financial Risk in a Day
Understand Bonds & Gilts in a Day
Understand Shares in a Day

Chapter One

Commodity Trading

A (Very) Short History

By the mid nineteenth century Chicago had already become a major trading centre in the United States, due to its railroad and telegraph connections with the East. Around the same time, in the 1840's, the McCormick reaper was invented to make the harvesting of wheat much easier. The result of this innovation was a vast increase in wheat production and more Midwest farmers travelling to Chicago to sell their produce. The dealers in the Windy City then shipped the wheat all over the country.

However, as Chicago grew in importance the storage facilities decreased, along with ways for weighing the goods. So the farmers and dealers got together to create a central facility where the two parties could meet and deal on "spot" grain - cash being swapped for immediate delivery of wheat.

Very soon the farmers and dealers began to commit themselves to exchanges of cash and wheat at some time in the future, say the farmer's next trip to the city. For example, the farmer (seller) would agree a price with a dealer (buyer) on the price for 1,000 bushels of wheat to be delivered in the month of August. This suited both parties since the farmer knew he had made a sale and how much he would make, whilst the dealer knew the price he would have to pay and so had time to arrange a profitable sale before receiving the wheat. At first these deals were made verbally and relied on both parties honouring the deal, but soon they began to exchange written contracts along with deposits.

As these contracts became more common, dealers started using them as collateral to obtain bank loans. Also dealers began buying and selling them between themselves as and when they had found a buyer for the wheat in other parts of the country. If a dealer had arranged to buy wheat in August but was struggling to find a buyer, he might sell the contract on to another dealer who had already arranged an end buyer.

On the other side of the fence, the farmers also began buying and selling their contracts based on their obligation to deliver the wheat. One farmer may have had a poor crop and found himself short of wheat, whilst another may have produced more than he had existing contracts for. A simple deal could then be put together to satisfy both farmers before they took their produce to the market.

Naturally the price of the contracts would fall and rise depending on what happened in the wheat market. Bad weather, for example, in the growing districts would make dealers prepared to pay more for their wheat since the supply would be lower. Similarly the farmers would hold out for more money for the same reason.

By the early 1850's people started buying and selling contracts in wheat who had absolutely no intention of ever taking delivery of or producing wheat.

> *The commodity speculator had been borne!*

Nowadays, there are trading exchanges all over the developed world which take in a diverse range of commodities from the naturally occurring, such as wheat, sugar and precious metals through to intangibles such as currencies, shipping rates and stock indices.

In order to be traded on modern commodity exchanges, a cash commodity must meet some basic conditions:

✔ The commodity's price should fluctuate by such a degree as to create uncertainty in the market. This forms the basis of the futures market by creating potential profit and risk.

✔ It must be standardised and in its raw state if an industrial or agricultural commodity. That is why you will find futures contracts for wheat but not flour.

✔ Any commodity which is perishable, must have an adequate shelf life to meet the deferred delivery of the 'future' contract.

The variety of different instruments and contracts available, denominated in several major currencies, and with a great variety of underlying commodities, means that the markets are fast moving and, in terms of their monetary size, absolutely enormous.

Hedgers

The Hedger is somebody who has a particular position in a physical commodity, and who is seeking to safeguard that position. The classic, and most historic example, might be the farmer. He begins a breeding cycle of cattle which involves his investment in bulls and heifers. He knows that a certain period will pass before the calves are born, can be reared, and eventually brought to market. During that time, of course, the world can change considerably, and any financial projections he might have made, and which made sense three years previously, may not do so at the time the cattle are ready for sale. Accordingly, he needs to arrange some sort of contract whereby the delivery of his commodity is guaranteed at a time in the future, and an agreed delivery price which gives him a certainty of profit, all other things being equal.

In commodities parlance, he is "physically **long** of beef". Hence, he would arrange a futures contract whereby he sold beef short in order to ensure a fixed price in the future.

Of course, you need not have a physical ownership of a commodity in order to hedge. For example, you might be the major producer of a chemical which must use silver in its processes. If so, you must fix the price of silver well in advance. Accordingly, you could "go long" in the market with a futures contract.

Traders

What really helps to drive the market, however, is the presence of Traders. They may have no physical position in any commodities whatsoever, but simply wish to exploit differences in supply and demand, or local currency differences in the value of a particular asset. This is known as **arbitrage**.

Imagine for example, a Trader who perceives that in the London market the price of a silver Futures contract for December delivery is fractionally lower than the equivalent contract in, say, Chicago. It might be possible for him to short one contract in one market with a simultaneous contract in another market and arbitrage on the difference. Alternatively, he might short one contract and long another, so that the overall effect is that each contract would cancel out the other, but there would be an arbitrage profit on the margin.

Hedgers -v- Traders

Some people run away with the idea that one party is bad for the market, but this is simply not true. **Traders provide a great deal of much needed liquidity** because of their willingness to trade in almost any commodity and in any contract format. However, **Hedgers have a genuine need to trade**, and it is generally thought that they will hold a position with more aggression than a Trader because they are more closely involved in the result. This gives a useful dimension to the market.

Gearing

Just like derivatives, the gearing effect is what makes commodities so interesting. This works in two ways. Later, when discussing how you get started in commodities trading, we will discuss margin and the way this allows you to trade in contracts worth more than the funds you have physically deposited with your broker.

But, perhaps the major source of gearing comes in the composition of the contracts themselves. The stock market is a good example of this.

Imagine you think the U.K. stock market will rise in the coming month. You might decide to invest £100,000 in an index tracking fund, and, if the market increases by 5%, you will have made £5,000 or so, not taking into account any costs. However, had you written a Futures contract, you could have made the same £5,000, but this would have been a 50% gain based on the £10,000 margin, which would underlie your trading account.

Of course, gearing works both ways. If the stock market falls in the first example, you still have £95,000 of your original stake money, and could exit with nothing more than a harsh lesson learned. But, if you had *sold* a Futures contract instead of buying one, then you would have lost £5,000, which, in this case, is half your original stake money! Had you not closed out your position in time, you could have lost even more. You would not last long in Futures behaving like that.

There is a "**double gearing**" aspect of Futures. Firstly that you are allowed to trade in much bigger quantities than your margin investment would suggest. And, secondly, movements on indices or Futures contracts can be dramatic in relation to that stake money, though not necessarily in relation to the market itself. Hence, with a relatively small stake, and without too much volatility, considerable money can be made.

Anatomy of a Trade

Whilst individuals who trade will do so for differing reasons, whether they are hedging, speculating or arbitraging, the basic make-up of a trade or series of trades will be the same. This is one of the most important features of trading in commodities or Futures:

> *You need to have a basic agreement on what*
> *a particular "contract" will include.*

For example, you might be happy to trade in a gold contract, but you will want to know the **quantity** of gold involved, the **delivery date**, the **price** and it's **purity**. All these features are set down in considerable detail by the various markets, and allow individuals to react quickly without ever having to think in depth about whether or not the "asset" in question is suitable.

People dealing in commodities will usually agree to buy or sell these standard quantities of specified assets on a particular future date, but at a price they agree now. The purpose of so doing for the hedger is to introduce a degree of certainty into an otherwise uncertain world (see *Risk Management Strategies* in *Understand Financial Risk in a Day* by Alex Kiam). The arbitragers and speculators however, are simply looking to exploit the uncertainty.

If someone buys a contract, then he is obliged to buy the asset on a particular date. If someone were to sell a commodities contract, then they would have to sell the particular assets in question on a particular date.

As always, an example is the easiest way of understand why anybody would do this.

Imagine you are a speculator and you think that the price of gold is about to rocket because of difficulties in the gold producing regions. You would probably buy a Futures contract and would therefore be taking a "long position". Let's say the current Future's prices of gold is £100 per contract (for easy reckoning). If, during the life of the contract, the price of the contract itself should rise to, say, £150, due to the perceived shortages actually becoming reality, then the contract holder would simply then sell his contract at £150 having made a handsome 50% profit.

Of course, should the price go the other way because of over-production, the speculator might find that he can now sell his contract for only £50, and thus would lose £50. The most successful traders recognise when events are going against them, and learn to close out positions that have gone wrong sooner rather than later (in the chapters that follow on how to create your own trading strategy, you will see that this is a crucial underlying principle of successful trading).

Apart from the profit motive in this trade, the speculator used a Futures contract rather than buying the hard commodity itself because it is far simpler to be the holder of an abstract paper contract, than the commodity itself. Imagine buying a commodity such as wheat, where would the trader store it, what would he do about insurance, what about transportation? By using these derivative contracts, these questions are not an issue.

It is important to understand that when you buy a Futures contract, the most you can actually lose is the total amount of your investment - £100 in the above example if gold should become worthless. This is, of course, highly unlikely, and you should have the opportunity to follow the price down and salvage at least some of your money on the way out. **Selling contracts in commodities on the other hand is far more dangerous, because the risk is almost unlimited.**

For example, imagine our speculator thought that huge amounts of gold were to be discovered and that this would halve the price. In this case, he would go out and sell the contract he bought in the previous example, for the same amount. He has now received £100 but he is obliged to make delivery of the gold on the specified date. Of course, he knows that gold will collapse in price, that he will be able to buy the contract to close out his position at £25, and will therefore make £75 profit.

However, imagine that matters go the other way. For example, all gold mines simultaneously discover that the gold they are mining today is the last they will ever discover. There is now a finite amount of gold available in the world and the price just spirals. Before the trader can act, the contract to close out his position costs him £1,000. When he buys the contract at £1,000 he has closed out his position completely but has lost 10 times his stake money! Such wild price fluctuations are not uncommon, particularly if you consider political instability in the Middle East which affects oil, or huge Stock Market crashes.

Selling short is therefore the most dangerous approach. When you buy long, you know that the price of the asset you have bought cannot fall below zero and so your total loss if you were to be unable to trade and miss the price collapse, would be the money you have expended (or the geared amount in relation to your margin).

But, by going short, you are obliged to deliver something you do not own and which you will therefore be obliged to buy whatever the price is. Prices can, theoretically, rise to infinity and so the risk of being wiped out by wild fluctuations is immense when selling short.

The Execution of a Trade

With so much to potentially gain or lose, the placing of an order is devastatingly simple once you are established with a trading account. Unlike major decisions like buying your home, or a new car, where there is a great deal of time consuming paperwork and inherent delays, the placing of commodities orders could hardly be simpler.

Imagine for example that you expect the price of oil to go down shortly. You will simply call your broker's trading desk and give your account number asking to sell one June oil contract at the market. Your broker should hold for a few seconds before confirming that the deal has been done. This will be executed directly to the relevant trading floor at the relevant commodities exchange either by computer or by telephone.

Your broker should then respond to the effect that you have sold one June oil contract at $YY per barrel.

That phonecall need take only a minute or so, but you are now on the hook for any potential rise in the price of oil. Imagine therefore that there is a shortage and oil begins to rise beyond the price that you have paid. You may see this as a long term trend and therefore wish to get out as quickly as possible. Accordingly, you telephone your broker and confirm that you would now like to buy one June oil contract at the market price. Once again, the deal can be done within a minute or so and you have now successfully closed your position, although you have lost money.

In fact, as the day goes on, you believe that the price of oil will continue to rise and so you call your broker again, wanting to go long by buying another June contract.

As the week wears on however, you realise that you were right in the first place and the price begins to slip, so that you have to call the broker yet again and sell short in order to close out the second position you created.

In this example, you may have spent only 10 minutes on the telephone, but you could have lost (or made) thousands of dollars.

Taking Delivery

If you take out a long position in some commodity and you choose not to close the position, or forget to do so, what happens? If you'd purchased six tonnes of Robusta coffee, would a couple of lorries appear in your road, and promptly tip out a mountain of caffeine on your drive the day after the contract expires? Sorry, but before you arrange coffee mornings for the next thirty years, this will not happen.

As your contract nears maturity, be it long or short, your brokerage firm will be keeping a wary eye on it. Some time before 'delivery' the firm will telephone all open long position holders and tell them to either close their position or prepare to take full delivery and also pay the value of the underlying contract. Similarly holders of open short contracts will be asked to close out their trades or make ready to deliver the underlying commodity (and show they have the required quantity & quality available for the delivery).

Even if you were to leave your position open in order to take delivery, you'll still not wake up to the aroma of freshly tipped coffee wafting from your garden. Instead you'll receive a receipt entitling you to get your commodity from a warehouse or suitable distribution point. Financial commodities are an exception to this rule.

> *Even manufacturers and processing companies who trade with the commodity rarely take delivery of the underlying goods.*

This is because the commodity contracts are not often in the exact quality or grade that they need. Instead they will close their position, having successfully hedged against price movements, and buy in the cash market. The cash market price will have followed the commodity price throughout the period in question. Only those companies who trade in a commodity for which they can find buyers of many different grades tend to take physical delivery.

Commodity Exchanges

Exchange floors are divided into Pits or Rings (shallow areas with raised steps around the edge) where traders stand facing one another. Each pit is designated for the trading of one or more commodity futures contracts.

At LIFFE (London International Financial Futures and Options Exchange) you will find pits for trading Coffee, White Sugar, Cocoa, Wheat, Barley, Potatoes and BIFFEX futures (see Appendix B)

All commodity exchanges work in a similar manner. The people trading in the pits must be members of the exchange itself. These members then support the exchange by paying dues and assessments. Ordinary individuals wishing to trade must do so through a broker who will employ officers who hold memberships.

The exchange not only supplies the place to make trades, but also ancillary services such as communication systems, price reporting and information circulation systems. Employees of the exchange will also keep an eye on the day-to-day operations and make sure the rules are strictly enforced. It does NOT set any commodity prices, or even buy or sell contracts itself.

Each Commodities exchange also has a clearing association which works with the exchange in a similar manner to the way a clearing house works with banks.

Well-capitalised members of the exchange and corporations or partnerships (one of whose officials must be a member of the exchange) make up the membership of the clearing association. Those members of the exchange who are not members of the clearing association, must clear their trades through those who are.

The association members must put up a fixed original margin with the clearing house. They also need to maintain the margin when price fluctuations go against them - with the clearing house able to call for additional margins through the day instead of waiting for the normal settlement at the end of the day.

Here are some of the major commodity exchanges around the world:

Australia

Sydney Futures Exchange (SFE)
30-32 Grosvenor St., Sydney, NSW 2000, Australia

Canada

Toronto Futures Exchange (TFE)
Two First Canadian Place, The Exchange Tower,
Toronto, Ontario M5X 1J2 Canada

The Winnipeg Commodity Exchange (WCE)
500 Commodity Exchange Tower, 360 Main St.,
Winnipeg, Manitoba R3C 3Z4 Canada

China

Beijing Commodity Exchange (BCE)
306 Chenyun Building, No. 8 Beichen East Road,
Chaoyang District, Beijing 100101 China.

France

Marche a Terme International de France (MATIF)
115 rue Reaumur, 75002 Paris, France.

Germany

DB (Deutsche Terminboerse) Postal address: 60284 Frankfurt,
Street address: Boersenplatz 7-11, 60313 Frankfurt, Germany.

Hong Kong

Hong Kong Futures Exchange Ltd. (HKFE)
5/F, Asia Pacific Finance Tower, Citibank Plaza,
3 Garden Road, Hong Kong.

The Stock Exchange of Hong Kong (SEHK)
1/F, One & Two Exchange Square, Central, Hong Kong

Japan

Chubu Commodity Exchange (C-COM)
(including Nagoya Textile Exchange, Nagoya Grain and Sugar
Exchange, Toyohasi Dried Cocoon Exchange)
2-15, Nishiki 3 Chome, Naka-ku, Nagoya 460, Japan.

Kansai Agricultural Commodities Exchange (KANEX)
1-10-14 Awaza, Nishi-ku, Osaka 550, Japan.

Kobe Rubber Exchange (KRE)
5-28, Kyutaro-machi 2-chome, Chuo-ku, Osaka 541, Japan.

Kobe Raw Silk Exchange (KSE)
126 Higashimachi, Chuo-ku, Kobe 650, Japan.

Osaka Textile Exchange
2-5-28 Kyutaro-machi, Chuo-ku, Osaka 541, Japan.

Tokyo Commodity Exchange (TOCOM)
14th Floor, S. Wing, Riverside Yomiuri Bldg.,
36-2 Nihonbashi-Hakozakicho, Chuo-ku, Tokyo 103, Japan.

Tokyo Grain Exchange (TGE)
(merged with Hokkaido Grain Exchange in 1995)
12-5 Nihonbashi Kakigara-cho, 1-chome, Chuo-ku,
Tokyo 103, Japan.

Tokyo International Financial Futures Exchange (TIFFE)
1-3-1 Marunouchi, Chiyoda-ku, Tokyo 100, Japan.

Malaysia

Kuala Lumpur Commodity Exchange (KLCE)
Fourth Floor, Citypoint, Dayabumi Complex, Jalan Sultan
Hishamuddin, P.O. Box 11260, 50740 Kuala Lumpur, Malaysia.

Netherlands

European Options Exchange (EOE-Optibeurs)
Rokin 65, 1012 KK Amsterdam, The Netherlands.

Financiele Termijnmarkt Amsterdam N.V. (FTA)
Nes 49, 1012 KD Amsterdam, The Netherlands.

New Zealand

New Zealand Futures and Options Exchange (NZFOE)
P.O. Box 6734, Wellesley St., 10th Level,
Stock Exchange Centre, Auckland, New Zealand.

Singapore

Singapore Commodity Exchange Ltd.
111 North Bridge Road #23-04/05, Peninsula Plaza, Singapore

Singapore International Monetary Exchange Ltd.
1 Raffles Place, No. 07-00, OUB Centre, Singapore

South Africa

South African Futures Exchange (SAFEX)
105 Central St., Houghton Estate 2198, P.O. Box 4406,
Johannesburg, 2000, Republic of South Africa.

United Kingdom

International Petroleum Exchange of London Ltd. (IPE)
International House, 1 St. Katharine's Way, London E1 9UN.

London International Financial Futures
and Options Exchange (LIFFE)
*(includes London Commodity Exchange - commodity products
began trading on LIFFE in 1996, following merger of the two
exchanges)*
Cannon Bridge, London EC4R 3XX.

London Metal Exchange (LME)
56 Leadenhall Street, London EC3A 2BJ.

OMLX, The London Securities and Derivatives Exchange
107 Cannon St., London

United States

American Stock Exchange (AMEX)
Derivative Securities, 86 Trinity Place, New York,
NY 10006, USA.

Chicago Board Options Exchange (CBOE)
400 S. LaSalle St., Chicago, IL 60605, USA.

Chicago Board of Trade (CBOT)
141 W. Jackson Blvd., Chicago, IL 60604-2994, USA.

Chicago Stock Exchange (CHX)
One Financial Place, 440 S. LaSalle St., Chicago, Ill. 60605-
1070, USA.

Chicago Mercantile Exchange (CME)
30 S. Wacker Drive, Chicago, IL 60606, USA.

Coffee, Sugar & Cocoa Exchange Inc.
4 World Trade Center, New York, NY 10048, USA.

Kansas City Board of Trade (KCBT)
4800 Main St., Suite 303, Kansas City, MO 64112, USA.

MidAmerica Commodity Exchange (MidAm)
141 W. Jackson Blvd., Chicago, IL 60604, USA.

Minneapolis Grain Exchange (MGE)
400 S. Fourth St., Minneapolis, MN 55415, USA.

New York Cotton Exchange (NYCE)
Four World Trade Center, New York, NY 10048, USA.

New York Mercantile Exchange
Includes NYMEX and COMEX divisions
Four World Trade Center, New York, NY 10048, USA.

New York Stock Exchange (NYSE)
11 Wall St., New York, NY 10005, USA.

Pacific Stock Exchange (PSE)
301 Pine St., San Francisco, CA 94104, USA.

Philadelphia Stock Exchange (PHLX), and
Philadelphia Board of Trade (PBOT)
1900 Market St., Philadelphia, PA 19103, USA.

Apart from the employees of the various exchanges monitoring
the operations and enforcing rules, there are several bodies
who supervise commodity trading. The most important of
these include:

Australian Securities Commission
Chifley Tower, Level 16, 2 Chifley Square, Sydney NSW 2001

Office of the Superintendent of Financial Institutions
255 Albert St., Ottawa, Ontario K1A 0H2, Canada

Commission des Operations de Bourse
39-43 Quai Andre-Citroen, 75739 Paris, France

Hessian Ministry of Economics, Transport and Urban and Regional Development and Exchange Supervisory Authority
Postfach 31 29, 65021 Wiesbaden, Germany

Securities and Futures Commission
11th-13th Floor, Edinburgh Tower, The Landmark
15 Queen's Road, Central Hong Kong

Ministry of Finance
3-1 Kasumigaseki, 1-chome, Chiyoda-ku, Tokyo 100, Japan

Commodities Trading Commission
Fifth Floor, City Point, Dayabumi , Jalan Sultan Hishamuddin
50050 Kuala Lumpu, Malaysia

Stichting Toezicht Effectenverkeer
Paleisstraat 1/P.O. Box 11723, 1012 RB/1001 GS
Amsterdam, Netherlands

Monetary Authority of Singapore
10 Shenton Way, MAS Building, Singapore 07911, Singapore

Securities and Futures Authority
Cottons Centre, Cottons Lane, London SE1 2QB, England

Commodity Futures Trading Commission
3 Lafayette Centre, 1155 21st St., Northwest, Washington, DC

Federal Reserve Board
20th St. and Constitution Ave. Northwest
Washington, DC 20551, USA

National Association of Securities Dealers
1735 K St. Northwest, Washington, DC 2000, USA

National Futures Association
200 W. Madison St., Suite 1600
Chicago, IL 60606-344, USA

Securities and Exchange Commission
450 Fifth St. Northwest, Washington, DC 2054, USA

Chapter Two

Before You Begin

With stories of fortunes to be made in a frighteningly short time and with a relatively small stake at the outset, many have made the mistake of rushing in to commodities trading without sufficient preparation. In this respect, commodity trading is no different from any other business enterprise. You must not only have a well thought out business plan, and be prepared to stick to it, but also have the maturity and flexibility to alter it if necessary.

How Much Money

The amount you can make trading commodities will be directly related to the margin you can deposit with your broker. There are varying views on what amount is a working minimum, but £20,000 seems to be a figure which is generally accepted as providing sufficient liquidity for the trader to take reasonable positions in diverse markets.

Risk Banding

Of course, an individual whose entire fortune consists of £20,000 in cash would perhaps be ill advised to consider commodities trading at all. In order to deal with the inevitable losses that will occur (against a hopefully positive trend of gains), you must be prepared to lose your entire stake if trades do not go the right way for you, even with various stop loss mechanisms and decisive cutting short of loss positions. Some argue that the amount used in commodity trading should be no more than 5% of an individual's overall net worth (i.e, all your assets less liabilities) or even no more that 5% of his liquid net worth. Whatever, **the message is clear - do not trade in commodities with money that you cannot afford to lose**.

Know Thyself

Some people simply cannot concentrate on a sedentary or cerebral game such as chess, needing the physical movement around a sports field in order to feel comfortable and bring out the best of their abilities. So it is with trading. Some people will be detail obsessed and perhaps lack dynamism.

These people should clearly choose a system which best suits that approach. Other traders might be "big picture" traders, who want to take strategic positions based on broad brush trends. Whatever, you must be comfortable with the approach you are going to take.

Practice Makes Perfect

In my days in stockbroking, I was often approached by younger members of the dealing team or administrative staff who were interested to hear my views because they had developed "a system". It might be based on only buying those shares where the directors are known to have made heavy purchases in the previous year. Or it might be one of confining their portfolio to consumer stocks or household names. On the other hand it might be more sophisticated and based on chart analysis. Whatever the basis of the system I always advised a protracted period of testing. No "safe" system can be conceived in the abstract and then tested the first time with real money.

So, for the private investor, as for the professional, practice trading is a must. Run your system for at least a year, which, in any event, will make you more expert at dealing with the various different unforeseen issues which can arise, and, at the same time, gather historical data to test that system with hindsight.

Of course, none of this means that you will definitely make money, because the world can change overnight, let alone over a couple of years. But, the exercise of practice trading could lead you to conclude that either your system does not work, or you are simply not cut out to trade. If so, that would be the most valuable lesson learned with little material cost.

> *The more successful you are,*
> *the more money you will lose!*

Facing Losses

There is a romantic myth about the trader who never loses. This is, of course, nonsense. Most top traders will agree that any ratio of wins over losses that exceeds 50:50 will make money. If you can get to 60:40 then you are likely to make a considerable amount. However, you will still face the 40% losses.

You must have the psychology whereby you are able to shrug off losses and treat them objectively as part of your overall system. You must learn to cut short those losses rather than waiting for improvement, and allow your profitable trades to run on. Many traders say that the real money they make is in judging when to close a profitable trade. It is the old adage from Lord Rothschild, "Always leave a little profit for the next man".

Systems -v- Trends

There is certainly a divide in markets throughout the world as to which traders follow trends, and which traders are system driven. Trends assume that everything about a market is known (collectively by the market), and therefore a particular movement in a any direction is part of a natural progression. It is difficult, however, to know when a trend has changed, or merely slowed down.

Alternatively, one can be system driven and use buying and selling signals or other arithmetical data to give an impetus to the closing or opening of a trade.

Chapter Five considers these issues in greater depth, but the reason for raising them now is not to make you choose at the outset, but simply to let you know that there is more than one approach which you might want to consider. No matter what approach a trader might use, he will also be fully aware of the strategies that other traders are implementing as they are likely to have an indirect effect on him. This is why you need to be aware of all the different approaches that are in widespread use.

Finding a Broker

Before you can trade at all, you will need a broker. How you choose one is largely up to you, and, clearly, personal recommendation is always the best route.

However, if you need to approach the matter cold, then a visit to the likely shortlist, and a little beauty parade should pay dividends. There are many key questions.

❑ Are you being taken seriously?
❑ Does the firm have the facilities to execute trades swiftly?
❑ If your contact is unavailable, who will cover for him?

At the end of the day, there is also a question of commission. Because costs are an important factor and there is unlikely to be any advice given, you might like to chose a firm with which you feel most comfortable, and which is also charging competitive rates.

Diversify

There are arguments both for and against diversification. For example, if you are simply focused on precious metals, or even one precious metal, you are likely to build up experience and knowledge more quickly. However, you will be completely exposed to some major event which could wipe you out entirely. The release of hitherto undiscovered gold reserves, hyper-inflation in a platinum producing economy, diseased herds or crops, the onset of war in an OPEC country, can all have very considerable effects on the trades you have opened. If you are diversified throughout several different markets, then you may be able to salvage the majority of your portfolio.

The Nine Major Factors

Before you ever give your first order, the nine factors below should be explored, understood and borne in mind.

1. Identify precisely the amount of money you are going to stake, having satisfied yourself it is money that you can actually afford to lose.

2. Identify the market in which you are going to trade and the particular contracts. You may wish to diversify or specialise, but you must be absolutely clear at the outset.

3. Understand yourself. You should have a reasonable understanding of how you react under pressure and in certain situations. Are you instinctive, or are you more detail orientated? Do you follow hunches and win, or must you look at every aspect of a problem before acting? By knowing how you are likely to react when the pressure is on and the money is at stake, you should be able to select the trading system to suit you.

4. Install external checks in your system. You should have discipline installed in your system, for example, alarms on your computer software, or points of action on your charts. This will prevent you from conceiving a system in the abstract, and then altering it as you go along.

    If you are not careful, and you do not adhere to the disciplines you created at the outset, you will turn yourself into a rogue trader, and your losses could magnify dramatically.

5. Control your costs. Costs are not crucial, as long as you are getting the service from your broker, and you are able to achieve what you want to. But, if you are not, then you might as well go to the cheapest discount broker. This is because sometimes your profits on trades will be very fine, and significant commissions could wipe them out. It is quite feasible that in the bad times, the only profit you make could be wiped out by costs.

6. Be ready for losses. This is very important. If you are not able to stand frequent and large losses, sometimes over long periods, either psychologically or financially, based on the amount you are trading, then you will be in trouble. Even the best trader will lose money for a very large proportion of the time, and you must not take this personally. Be ready for it, and simply deal with it.

7. Cut short your losses. If you see a position you have worsening, then do not be afraid to crystallise the loss. By so doing, you will actually limit that loss.

8. Let your profits run. Similarly, if you are making profits, then you will want to ensure that you capture them, but do not get jittery, and close out successful positions too quickly. You must let the profits run to your pre-set limits. Once again, this is all down to discipline.

9. Remain objective. Even if you become the most successful trader in the world, Mr 100% who cannot go wrong, then remain objective. Let other people take a romantic view, let others talk about you as infallible. At all times, recognise your own frailty, and the fact that you must be experiencing particular luck to do as well as you are.

Fraud and Commodity Trading

You may have, by now, decided that you are really attracted to commodity trading, recognise the opportunity which it offers, but at the same time, having read this book and carried out a psychological profile, you might prefer to delegate the issue. This would involve instructing a professional firm and whilst all the advice in this book would be of use to you in helping you to evaluate any firms you might wish to instruct, there is one big issue of which you must be aware - fraud.

You have read how even the most experienced traders can get into deep water, executing trades which they cannot hope to cover. However, there is another form of fraud which is of more than academic interest to those reading this book.

This involves those 'advisors' who claim to be able to help make you make packet by investing your money.

- They have persuasive arguments.
- They are closer to the market than you can ever be.
- They control vast sums of money which allows arbitrage opportunities.
- They have legitimate inside information.
- They have combined experience greater than yours.
- They can more than justify their commissions by the profit they make.

Of course, one might then wonder why they are having to spend their evenings telephoning people for business. The least sinister of these scams involve genuine novice traders looking to build up a client base. In this case you will be

> *There's little doubt that trading on the world's commodity markets is fraught with danger due to price volatility. The possibility of fraudulent behaviour by individuals and corporations just makes the whole situation a lot more difficult to call.*

exposed to their incompetence and will be allowing them to practise with your money.

In the worst case, however, you may be committing your funds to someone who doesn't even intend to trade at all - they are simply going to lose your money in labyrinthine accounting systems which make it impossible to trace or regain. The blatant offenders just steal it, the less blatant are happy to produce a schedule of bogus trades which appear to have lost money when really, they never took place.

We are not talking small beer here at all. A recent case in North America involved $100 million. It was based on the time-honoured scam of repaying those who wanted to get out with the money contributed by new investors. Of course, those who 'made' money were the best salesmen, they had experienced it for themselves and so were happy to recommend relatives and friends, many of whom will now be left penniless. Remember, if someone is unregistered then you will not be covered by any investor compensation scheme.

There have been many convictions over the years in cases where individual traders have been able to defraud hundreds of investors over several years and lose literally millions of pounds.

What you can do

Of course, the rogue operatives are vastly outnumbered by the genuine traders who will make sincere attempts to trade for you. You simply have to establish who they are. As always, personal recommendation will be a good starting point and you should compile a short list in this way if you can. Once you have decided on the two or three best firms for you, perhaps on their brochure, facilities and the way they have treated your enquiry, you need to ask the following key questions;

✔   What regulatory organisation does the firm belong to?

✔   Are there any independent references, either from happy clients or from banks etc.?

✔   Can the investment house in question confirm how their banking arrangements work, especially as to client money?

✔   Who owns the firm?

✔   How long has the investment house been trading, and what is the concrete proof of their results? Don't accept any guff about client confidentiality - they either have successful accounts they can show you, or they don't.

✔   Do they confine their trades to recognised and registered exchanges. Or are they dealing outside such structures, directly with counterparties, who may or may not have the financial strength to deliver.

If you stick to this approach you should be able to weed out most of the dangerous and dishonest operators, but remember, it is your money and no-one will ever treat it as carefully as you do.

Market Fraud?

Can the commodity markets be manipulated to the benefit of some players and the detriment of others? Certainly Nick Leeson and Mr 5%, Yasuo Hamanaka, believed they could move the markets - and the reality is that they probably could. We now know that these two cases involved so-called 'rogue traders', but are other people influencing markets to their own ends and using their own money? If they are, then it could be argued that their activities are no less fraudulent than those of the blatant scam merchants.

In a recent case, which almost went to court, an options trader lost $164,000 when silver prices rose by 70% in six months. He believed that the market had been 'altered' by some of the larger players who had bought several million ounces of the precious metal. The basis of the alleged conspiracy was that prices had been raised by moving silver out of warehouses monitored by the COMEX division of the New York Mercantile Exchange , and into London bullion houses where inventories are not publicly reported.

Chapter Three

Trading Strategies

Getting your trading strategy right is absolutely crucial. There are enough external reasons for you to lose money, unforeseen market movements, mistakes, market manipulation and so on. To also lose money because you do not understand the market, have not fully worked out, or do not adhere properly to your own trading system, is to stack the odds so far against you, as to make it impossible for you to succeed.

It has been estimated that as many as eight out of 10 of those who trade in commodities end up as net losers.

Clearly, with competition so intense, you must be absolutely clear as to your objectives and the method of achieving them.

General Rules

This chapter will contain a great deal of detailed information, and outline one or two strategies for you, along with specific methods and approaches such as carousel arbitrage, or the Egyptian ratchet. But, before moving on to detail, there are some very important principles which you should understand and consider employing.

Trend Trading/Following a Trend

There is considerable debate amongst commodity traders as to whether or not Trend Trading is the only way forward, the major way forward, or one of many. Perhaps it's opposite is Day Trading. With Day Trading, you are trying to make money by opening and closing positions on the day. This is, of course, very difficult, but also psychologically intensive. If you do not make money that day, you will feel unhappy, and perhaps under greater pressure the next day.

With more gradual trends, things are easier. For example, I used to value my personal Stock Market portfolio on a daily basis, simply because I could do so by pressing a button on my client computer system. Of course, for three days a week it would go up, but for two days a week it would go down. This gave me two miserable days a week. However, as I became busier with clients' affairs I would value it only once a month. Now it has risen 11 months out of 12 and fallen only once. I have only one miserable day a year!

This is the difference between Day Trading and Trend Trading. If you look at Stock Markets, commodities markets or indeed any other market, there will be fluctuations. If each daily or even hourly fluctuation is going to mean a loss or a profit for you, to be crystallised, then you will be under intense pressure and suffer as a result.

Cut Short your Losses

It has already been said, but since it is so important it needs re-iterating. You have to understand that no matter how sophisticated your system, no matter how diligently you stick to it, you will always face losses. They are an inherent part of commodity trading. Successful traders have learned to accept them for what they are. Accordingly, if you are facing a loss:

●   Do not be afraid to close it out,
●   Do not be afraid to lose money,
●   Do not be afraid to admit that you were wrong.

You can easily convince yourself that things will change, and that the position will become positive. But, this is the road to damnation. You should also ensure that your broker allows you to place automatic closing orders so that you do not get a second chance at making the decision to close out your losses.

Perhaps a golf analogy will help you to understand why losses are important. Imagine you are in a stroke play tournament against another player. If you are level on strokes, and at the 13th hole you take 13 shots, where he takes 3, you are now 10 shots behind, and, presumably, will find it very difficult to catch up and win the game.

However, in a match play tournament, you are playing per hole. Hence, you might halve the first 15 holes, take an unheard of 20 shots on the 16th, but go on to win the 17th and 18th by 1 stroke. In that case, you have won the match despite having taken far more strokes than your opponent. It is also the basis of successful commodity trading.

It does not matter if you make a loss here or there, or even eight of the 18 golf holes, so long as you win the other 10. The analogy may seem imperfect because if you are wiped out by taking a triple bogey on the 5th hole, you may not continue the match. However the commodity parallel to this is when you face a "margin call".

Let Your Profits Run

Another sign of inexperience in trading commodities is to snatch at a profit as soon as it is there. Lord Rothschild used to say "It is never wrong to take a profit" and there is a certain wisdom in that. However, you must allow your profits to run because the way that commodity trading generally pans out, you will need the big profits to make up for the many smaller losses. So, if you limit the profits, you may not be able to get the balance right.

The problem you face is that you may have an exit price on a particular contract and reach it. However, you may be quite convinced that the way things have developed, you should let the contract run. The danger of letting it run, however, is that it might suddenly turn the wrong way and you will have failed to exit at your pre-arranged price, and your whole trading strategy may collapse.

So, have your broker arrange a "**trailing stop**". This is, effectively, an arrangement which will follow the price of your contract as it continues to rise (after it has exceeded your exit price), but, should it reverse it's direction, it will effectively "meet" the trailing stop and close out the bargain. This is a highly effective and very important means of allowing you to squeeze extra profit out of contracts that turn out to be more successful than you had even anticipated.

Psychology

With very few exceptions, traders come to the commodity market with some sort of history. Of course, your history need have nothing to do with commodities or other financial markets.

Maybe you are the youngest in a family of seven children, and have been used to being knocked about. Maybe as an only child, you have been used to being allowed a lot of latitude from your parents. Other positive and negative experiences that you may have had will be reflected in your approach to commodity trading. What you must ensure, is that you do the thinking and the therapy in advance, rather than afterwards!

For example, when I first came to market trading, my attitude was pretty robust. If I lost, it simply made me more determined. However, a colleague of mine had to win all the time, or it simply consumed him with anger and self-recrimination. Hence, three or four bad trades from him and he was effectively excluded from success as a commodity trader because his psychology would not allow him to make objective decisions.

Interestingly, my own sang froid, has been tested on many occasions, and I have to confess that it has it's limits. If I lose large enough for long enough, then eventually my confidence becomes eroded. Far from reacting like the rogue trader who believes he is invincible, I begin to worry. Is my system really good, or have I discovered a flaw? Is it me? Am I working too hard? What am I missing? Am I getting older? Am I simply losing my competitive edge against younger, hungrier traders?

It is at that point that I have to withdraw and allow the systems to take over entirely. By doing so, the systems will gradually right themselves, and my psychology will improve. Each time this happens, I sit down subsequently and laugh at how silly I have been for doubting myself. But, at the time it happens, there are significant sums at stake. Over the years, I have recognised that this is my make-up, and have put in procedures to prevent it causing any disasters.

You must do the same. You must ask those around you to give an indication of how they think you are.

❑ Are you highly competitive?

❑ Do you want public recognition, or are you much quieter?

❑ Do you need the buzz of colleagues in order to bounce ideas off them, or are you able to study quietly on your own free from distractions?

❑ Are you a big picture individual who tends to draw the important concepts from a situation, or are you more concerned with the detail of what actually happens?

You really must build up some sort of basic profile of yourself before you can decide what approach is likely to be the best for you.

Risk Profiling

Clearly, you will need to decide the level of risk you are taking. For example, you may decide to use no more than 5% of your net wealth in commodities, and in the event that it is lost, abandon commodities altogether. You might therefore consider this to be compatible with a very high risk strategy, for example, shorting contracts in volatile commodities. Alternatively, you may be taking a long view and using a large proportion of your net worth, and so you do not require such immediately dramatic results.

We have already seen how going short or going long will have a different level of ultimate risk. Of course, the commodities in which you trade will also have different risk profiles. You will need to research and talk to other traders and advisors in order to discover what commodity is likely to produce the type of volatility you would like. With grain for example, we tend to know where it is, and where it is being grown, moreover we have very advanced processes for its production and storage, but, at the end of the day, we are left with the vagaries of the climate. Conversely, production of gold, silver or oil is largely unaffected by the weather, but political factors can be more significant. You will need to decide which commodities suit you.

Finally, you will need to decide whether or not you are going to diversify. Perhaps your portfolio will include the naturally occurring commodity, such as gold or oil, but also some intangibles such as stock indices. Generally, as you carry out your research it should become clear to you which is likely to give you the most satisfaction.

Realism

Everybody must acknowledge that the markets are random. Even when trends can be predicted, they essentially represent the ordered chaos of modern living. Never be surprised, and never give up if the whole canvas on which you are trying to create your masterpiece, is suddenly changed beyond recognition. Learn to accept this for what it is, another major opportunity from which you can make more money.

Making a Plan

It is unwise to approach the commodities market without a very clear plan. This plan need not be very complicated, but it must be clear. For example, your plan should be capable of summary in a sort of mission statement. It might say *"I will go long in oil on six month delivery dates using trailing stops for rising profits, and cutting losses at points agreed with the broker when sales are executed. I will never trade in more than 10 contracts at once or $X Thousand, which ever is the greater. I will not sell short."*

Alternatively, your statement might read *"I will trade in set quantities of grain and soya across several exchanges with the aim of producing arbitrage profits. I will use stop loss mechanisms when I sell short. If long, I will not use trailing stops, but simply my own judgement. Trading in trends, I will therefore use longer contracts where applicable."*

By having an overall strategy such as this, you will be able to refer to it in times of stress and difficulty and then evaluate the action you are about to take to see if it is consistent with your overall requirements.

Specific Trading Strategies

Once you have got your general approach right, and have learned your basic principles, you will need specific strategies. Many successful traders do not make their strategies known. They guard them jealously because they want to have exclusive use. Others, once they have made money, like to talk about what they do and how they do it.

Whilst there are various common tricks, such as spread trading, or "tarantula trading", other systems are more arcane. The sections below deal with some of them.

Spread Trading

Spread trading simply means that you are going long and short in similar Futures contracts at the same time. You expect one of the contracts to move more quickly than the other and this will narrow or widen the price spread between them. This is how you will profit. Imagine for example, two markets as showing differing prices for the same contract. There may, of course, be a legitimate market reason for this but you may also believe the difference could be overstated and that it offers a chance for profit.

Another opportunity will arise if there is some sort of fundamental movement in the market itself. For example, if you think that the demand for meat is going to move significantly between one delivery date and the next, there will be the opportunity of a spread. If you think that there is going to be increased demand for the new meat, then you would go long in the close (shortest dated) contracts, and go short in the furthest (longest dated new delivery contracts). This will be called a bull spread. But, if you thought that the new meat would not face the same demand for some reason, then you would short the close contract and purchase the more distant one, which would be called a bear spread.

A major reason for spreading is that the margin money required is slightly lower, and therefore increases your gearing, which makes more efficient use of your capital. Additionally, if you are wrong when writing a bull or bear spread, then one half of your bargain will rise, although not quite as far as the value of the other side will fall, but at least your overall loss is somewhat limited by having set up this inter-relationship between the two bargains.

Tarantula Trading

Imagine you go long in oil with a 12 month delivery date and you pay $100 per contract (to use a fictitious price). If, after 3 months, the price is $130 per contract, then you are clearly in the money. However, in the absence of a trailing stop or other instruction, were the price to fall dramatically, then you could easily find yourself at month six facing a price of $90. At that point (notwithstanding that you have six further months) your strategy seems to have temporarily failed. If you now short the same number of contracts at $90 you will ensure that your loss cannot exceed the $10 differential (all other things being equal).

However, if you still believe in the oil price rise, you might buy a further contract, once again, at $90. You are now long of two sets of contracts, and short with one. If the oil price should now rise dramatically, to say, $150 per barrel, then you will face delivery on the contract you shorted, which you can make through the second contract you purchased, and the first contract will once again show you the profits you required.

This is a basic principle of the trading model known as Tarantula Trading. In this case, you construct a spider with any number of "legs" or contracts. The central body of the spider is the expiry date of the various commodities contracts you have, and they should all be a consistent delivery date, of say, December. The beginning of each spider's leg will be the purchase of the relevant contracts, and time will expire from the end of the spider's leg into the spider's body.

If, at any point, your long contract should show a loss position, then the spider's leg is said to be broken. Of course, you can leave it broken and do nothing about it because, as time continues to expire towards the body, the oil price may improve and the spider's leg may "heal". Alternatively, you may short the position to close out the loss. The leg is not healed, because you are still losing money. However, you would now start a second spider's leg as in the oil example above, where you might go long again, but at a different price. If the price of oil then recovers, your second leg will be in profit, and you can either let it run, or place a matching short on that leg, (most traders prefer to let it run).

You could now construct your third leg or indeed all subsequent legs, depending on how you view the various positions. By carefully creating a series of legs which are either still "open" or which have been shorted out, you can gradually ensure that within certain narrow price ranges your losses are minimised, but you are likely to receive a profit.

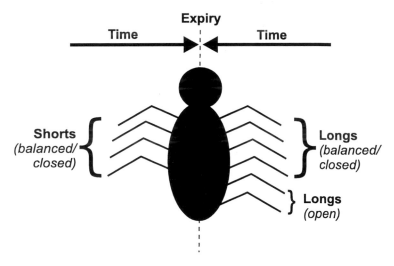

If, for example, you have six legs which are no longer open, but two which are, and they have been opened at the low-est prices during the trading cycle, then even if the oil price recovers only to the level at which it began, you will make very considerable profit on the two open legs. The other six will simply be balanced positions and (other than for trading costs), will be neutral.

Of course, the constraints of eight legs, whilst entirely appropriate for contracts in, say, eight major currencies, may not suit everyone. Some more complicated models may be required, where the "legs" are of differing time-scales as well as prices and contracts. In this case, they may be presented as a spider's web or "cobweb". Sophisticated computer programmes are necessary to keep track of web trading. And, it is useful to have diagrammatic representation on screen which is constantly updated as prices change, and will give the trader advanced warning of likely web failures.

Pyramid Trading

Imagine oil is $100 a contract. You go long in one contract, and the price immediately falls to $80. At that point you go long again, but in this case, with two contracts. On the first contract you will need oil to rise above $100 in order to be in profit, but on the second contract you will need it to rise only above $80.

Your break-even price, therefore, for the three contracts is actually $86.66 per contract. At that point you could close the trade and exit. Had you bought only one contract at $80, then your exit price would have been $90, and if you had bought three, then your exit price would have been $85.

If the price continues to fall further, you might then buy more contracts, say, a further four at $70, and then a further five at $60. The point of this is that you gradually create a pyramid of contracts with different exit prices. If you are right about your initial belief that $100 was a sensible price at which to go long, and the price does reach $100 plus, then the profit you make on the subsequently purchased contracts at $80, $70 and $60 will be immense.

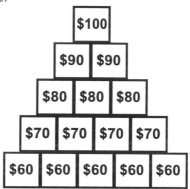

Of course, you need not close out positions as the price rises (although it might be wise to do so, or at least run trailing stops), you might in fact continue to buy, still in the belief that the price will far exceed your original expectation of $100. In this case, a diagrammatic representation of your strategy would not be pyramid or triangular shaped, but diamond shaped.

Carousel Arbitrage

This is potentially a very complicated trading strategy because, like the spider's web, a trader can choose any number of legs, although in reality, the availability of contracts and delivery dates is likely to be the limiting factor.

The carousel may be used in a variety of ways, but perhaps the simplest to understand is the spread trader's carousel. Imagine a carousel with, say, eight horses on the outer ring and eight on the inner ring. If each outer horse represents a long contract, and each inner horse represents a short contract, (particularly for different delivery dates), then each pair of horses is effectively a spread. As the carousel spins (time elapses), the relationship of each horse changes in that one rises and one falls.

Let's imagine that we have eight different contracts in, say, liquid propane, orange juice, soya bean oil, wheat, live cattle, pork bellies and coffee. If the carousel is a bull spread carousel, the trader will have gone long in the outer horses (representing the old crop or production) and shorted the inner horses (representing the new crop or production). If he is right, then the short of the new crop will rise in value, but the long in the old crop will actually fall. Whilst the profits will be depressed by having lost money on one set of contracts, it will have made more than enough on the other contracts.

The expertise comes in judging when, as the carousel spins, (time elapses), the relationship of the inner and outer horses is such that contracts can be successfully closed at a profit. By cutting any losses short (if price movements are particularly against you), but letting profitable relationships between the horses run, it is possible to accumulate considerable profits on a successfully run carousel.

Further, if one set of horses is effectively closed out at a profit, you can re-invest the profit by creating a further relationship with two replacement horses, although as time elapses, the price relationship between each contract may not be beneficial, plus the fact that you are then failing to follow the trend, and are moving closer towards day trading. It is quite possible to lose all the profit made on a long term carousel with one or two ill-judged short term trades towards the end.

Three Dimensional Chess

In the popular television programme, Star Trek, Mr Spock is often seen playing the cerebral and challenging game of Three Dimensional Chess. With his dispassionate and logical approach, and his ability to adhere to rules without emotion, he would surely have made an excellent commodities trader.

It may not be surprising therefore that there is a trading strategy based on this three dimensional chess. Conventional chess based trading strategies did not allow for alterations in the delivery dates of various contracts. Similarly Tarantula Trading exhibits the same problems, in that the legs would all reach the body at a set delivery date.

If a trader's position changed in a commodity but he could still correct it by trading even longer (or shorter) then conventional models such as the Tarantula, or a simple 360 degree carousel, would be insufficient to express the complicated relationships which would evolve within the traders various strategies. Three dimensional chess provides the answer.

On the central of the three chess boards are the original delivery dates. Accordingly, they might be for June. Imagine, once again, that the oil contract is $100 for June delivery. If the oil price drops dramatically, then the trader may believe that he should go long again, in order to average out.

However, there is the danger that the price may not recover in time for June. He is best advised, therefore, to close out his June positions on the central chess board and then move to the higher (or longer board), and then set up similar contracts but with a longer delivery date. Assuming there was some volatil-

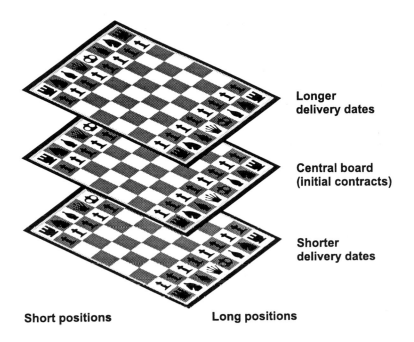

Longer delivery dates

Central board (initial contracts)

Shorter delivery dates

Short positions   **Long positions**

ity before the expiry of the central board contracts, then the exercise could be repeated on the bottom (or shorter) board. This is a very simple method of balancing positions over differing timescales. The art comes into the exercise when a trader successfully transfers liabilities between the various different delivery dates, i.e. from board to board. By continually re-rating the boards as each one is "cleared" the three dimensional chess approach can be ongoing with no need to close down the game overall.

Chapter Four

Who Got It Wrong

What makes commodities trading so exciting for the public bystander, is the twists and turns of volatile markets. This may all hinge in psychology, with the Schadenfreude complex, but there is no denying that to see one man go from a standing start to being a multi-millionaire and then be wiped out in a matter of days carries with it a hint of Shakespearean tragedy. The analogy is particularly strong when the fatal flaw exhibited by Shakespearean tragic heroes is not far from the mistakes of self knowledge made by those who are wiped out in derivatives markets.

This section therefore is intended as a warning to those who begin to trade successfully. Never forget that there have been many in the past who thought they had the perfect system, the perfect psychology or were just plain lucky, and discovered that none of those were the case. Perhaps everyone ought to come back and re-read this section on a regular basis before placing orders!

Sumitomo Copper

The global **copper** market is a billion dollar derivatives market. It is run through the **London Metal Exchange** and the most recent scandal involves Sumitomo, one of Japan's larger banking organisations. The allegations surround Yasuo Hamanaka, who has tried to explain the loss of $2.6BN as a result of alleged "rogue trading".

Rogue trading is not confined to copper, or indeed to derivative markets. It most often arises when an individual has a series of highly successful trades followed by a dull period. During the dull period, the trader tries to disguise his "temporary" lack of success by settling failed deals through some account which is not immediately apparent to settlement staff or auditors.

Of course, they fully intend to square the position once their "luck", judgement, or whatever returns. The belief is that no-one will be any the wiser, and it is likely that many rogue traders have managed this successfully. But, what often happens is that the individual digs himself in deeper. This may be because he has to trade more and more contracts at higher levels because he no longer has to make just today's profit, but has to make up for yesterday's loss. If he makes further losses, then the whole things just spirals.

Hamanaka, was known as Mr Five Percent, because he was thought to control up to 5% of the world's annual production of copper, although he was, allegedly, responsible for certain deals which involved as much as 10%. Whilst allegations include forgery, false payments and false accounting, what really worried the copper market was the overhang, or consequences, of Hamanaka's manipulation. If he really did control so much of the copper market, then who was going to be able to "unwind" all of his positions. To do so could produce a massive sell-off which would depress the market for months or even years, and put many producers out of business.

Perhaps what really happened is that those who own the underlying copper, either directly or via contracts, closed ranks and held their positions for now. The danger was, and perhaps still is that as soon as someone is forced to break cover, there could be a global sell-off with many traders fearing a bloodbath. Some traders predict a 20% fall in the price of copper itself could happen. But this would translate into falls of a 100-fold for those with the wrong market positions. Those who have written commodities contracts guaranteeing to buy copper at it's current price, (those with long positions), will be forced to complete those transactions, paying well over the odds to those on the other end of the bargain.

When you consider that in addition to all the other risks in commodity trading, there is a risk that powerful people might be loading the dice through false accounting, then the odds become even more worrying.

The Man Who Broke the Bank

Perhaps the most dramatic of all the recent scandals involving derivatives and commodities trading, is surely that of Barings Bank and it's alleged rogue trader, Nick Leeson. In this case, losses were accumulated on a previously unknown scale, and Mr Leeson's subsequent sudden disappearance, with accusations of the bank having been brought down by a conspiracy of Far Eastern businessmen, added a bizarre aspect to the fiasco.

Barings Bank was one of the best names in the city of London. A blue-blooded bank whose history went back to the 18th Century, and whose charitable works through the Baring Foundation were the envy and admiration of many. Years ago, the bank had been considered to be one of the great powers in the world, controlling such a large proportion of the world's finance that they were able to fund Government activities, and contribute greatly to the development of trade and the industrial revolution. With such a reputation, and still largely in private hands, many thought they were invincible.

Nick Leeson was a 28 year old trader from Watford, England. He had left school after having failed 'A' Level Mathematics, and went to work in the city. At first, his responsibilities were relatively minor, support roles in the settlement system. Whenever a deal is transacted, there is a significant electronic or paper trail behind it which needs to be managed. This is know as the back office. Leeson's experience was as a settlements clerk in the Baring's back office, and his detailed understanding of settlement was later to be of considerable assistance in the trades he carried out.

However, like many support staff in the city of London during the 80s, Leeson had ambitions. He saw himself as a glamorous trader in derivative markets, when the opportunity to go to Singapore came, Leeson took it. Once in Singapore he worked as a clerk at Simex, the **Singapore International Monetary Exchange**. He was generally thought to be good at his job and was therefore given increased responsibilities. Based on his experience, Barings managed to get Leeson a trading licence. Over the ensuing months, Leeson was recognised as a very talented and skilled trader. By 1993, he was the general manager of the Baring Futures in Singapore.

As time went by, Baring Singapore became increasingly successful. In only 7 months to July 1994, the Singapore trading activities provided a profit of $30M, almost 20% of the entire

Barings Group profit for the whole of the previous year. But, there were those that had their doubts. Some saw Baring's activities as the well controlled visions of a bank with exceptional staff - leaders in their fields. Others saw Baring's growing confidence as dangerous, and began to be at first amazed, and then alarmed, by the size of the positions they took. Barings had several major strategies based on the two most important **Simex Futures** contracts.

These were based on the Nikkei 225 Stock Market Index, and the Japanese Government Bond Future. Over the years, the trading in these contracts had moved away from Tokyo to Osaka, in the south of Japan, and also to Singapore. This allowed identical contracts to be traded in the three different centres at different prices based on market conditions and currency exchange. Even though the difference in these prices was tiny, it would, nonetheless, be significant if dealing frequently, on a geared basis, and in large volumes. The five strategies which Barings employed were as follows:-

Inter-Exchange Arbitrage

Under this system, contracts would be purchased or sold in both Singapore and Tokyo, or Osaka. All the contracts would be matched so that no open positions were left, and the profit would simply be made by the **arbitrage** between the fractional price movements. As members of both Osaka and Singapore exchanges, Barings were able to access information on both markets at once.

Taking Positions

When an organisation is as powerful as Barings, it will know what other market traders are doing. It will be able to use it's immense capital to squeeze out the smaller traders who may be forced to sell at a loss, because they just do not have the money to hold their positions overnight.

Spread Price Differentials

This allowed Barings to make money on the difference between the prices quoted for "Spreads", i.e. several contracts expiring on different dates, and prices quoted for the individual contracts in each different market.

Liquidity Arbitrage

There is greater liquidity in the Osaka derivatives market than in Singapore. So, given the amount of trades which Barings was effecting, it could allow it's clients to combine the better prices from Singapore with the greater liquidity from Osaka.

Large Order Arbitrage

Market knowledge would tell Barings of a large unfulfilled order in one market. This would then allow them to build up their own position in another market. During the day, as new of the large order in the other market became public, the price would move as a result of sentiment, thus allowing Barings to close out their smaller deal at a profit.

It is clear that in the early days, Barings were carrying out these trades very successfully, but, in January 1995, it appears that someone in the bank introduced a new trading strategy. They started to sell put and call options on the Nikkei 225 Index, receiving the premium for writing those options, and allegedly putting the proceeds into an unauthorised trading account, numbered **8888**, significant to the superstitious local community.

By writing both put and call options, struck at the same exercise price, Barings was creating a straddle. This is a bet on stability in the market, that it will not rise significantly, nor fall significantly. As long as the market remains within the trading range of the straddle, the bank pockets the profits on the option premiums and is never exercised. Barings would have been delighted to see the index stay in the narrow range between 19,000 and 21,000 points. Because this was the trading region, where the derivatives contracts would not be exercised, and the option premiums could simply be pocketed. Against this background, they continued to make a profit.

The bank, apparently, also expected a new year rally which often happens in Stock Markets, but this failed to materialise. As a result, the index fell to the lower end of Baring's expected trading range. But they were still ahead. However, in the early hours of January 17th, an enormous **earthquake** hit Japan's industrial centres of Kobe and Osaka. This was one of the largest earthquakes for years, and was bound to affect the market. At first the market fell down to around 19,000 points, just at the bottom end of Baring's safe trading range. However, matters got worse.

On 23rd January, the Nikkei 225 dropped down to 17,950 points. Barings faced a dilemma. They were now well out of the money and began heavy buying of March and June 1995 Futures contracts. The pressure was on. Barings had to cover their positions. The bank was about to make a massive bet that things would improve and that they would come out ahead, once again, as king of the traders. However, the market slid further, down to 17,605 points, and this left Barings with an estimated loss of some £380M. One of the theories was that Barings or someone within the bank was trying to single-handedly move the market. When a bank or trader is so powerful and deals with such numbers, they can often move the market with major trades. This sentiment was stronger after the earthquake and continued to keep the market down.

As time went by, it became harder and harder for the bank. They were holding massive positions which the whole market now knew about, and yet they were suppressed in an error account. Sooner or later the market would either move back up to the bank's trading range and rescue them, or time would run out. But, soon the news was out, both in the local market and internationally.

Barings had lost an amount possibly exceeding £800M, which was more than the bank's available capital. Barings Singapore activities had broken the entire bank. In the city of London, all was gloom. It had always been expected that the Bank of England would step in to shore up a major banking institution that was going bust. But, on this occasion, that decision was not made and the bank was allowed to go down. Institutions then rallied round with a view to buying the bank, which was soon sold to the ING Group.

The parallels with the Colombo scandal are illuminating. Once again, an alleged rogue trader, whether it be a branch of a bank or and individual trader, it doesn't matter, perhaps built up too great a belief in their own invincibility and began to take bigger and bigger positions.

Perhaps the resignation letter that Mr Leeson is alleged to have left on his desk says it all...."*It was never my intention to aim for this to happen, but the pressures, both business and personal, have become too much to bear, and have affected my health to the extent that a breakdown is imminent".*

Bre-x Minerals Ltd.

Early in 1997 another major news story broke surrounding commodities. This one had a slightly unusual flavour, as it did not involve rogue traders, or investors taking overweight positions.

BRE-X minerals Ltd was a small mining company with a very high profile **gold mining** project at Busang. Cores taken from the site showed unheard-of densities of gold which would make it a principal source of the precious metal. And there was always the prospect of the whole area being rich in the metal and becoming a major gold producer. A great many private and corporate investors were involved with this project via their holdings of Bre-x paper, and commodity prices were influenced by the potential arrival of new supply.

Sadly for those investing in the project, it turned out that the cores had been tampered with before testing and they didn't contain any gold at all. And to make matters worse, there were some fairly unsavoury goings-on behind the scenes, culminating in the chief geologist 'falling' from a helicopter above the site!

As usual in these cases, there was panic selling and the share price of BRE-X Minerals Ltd fell from a high of $26 in September 1996, to a low of $3 in April 1997, wiping millions off the paper value of the company. With some 214 million shares in issue, this amounts to losses of over $4 billion!

What made the scandal resonate throughout the investment markets of the world was the holders of the stock and their identities. As the shares had recently become part of one of the Canadian Stockmarket benchmark indices, it had necessarily become a holding for so-called low risk index-tracking funds.

Not only that, but many of the major shareholders in BRE-X stock were American Mutual Funds. Many names have been linked to holding or having sold the stock including The Bank of Montreal, The National Trust Company, and Invesco's Canadian arm.

Black Gold Metallgesellschaft

Metallgesellschaft is one of Germany's largest and most respected companies. In the late 1980s it decided to diversify by buying an oil company. The merits is this as a commercial decision have, however, been somewhat obscured by the resulting derivatives style catastrophe which took place.

Clearly, the management of Metallgesellschaft were concerned about **oil prices**. In an effort to buy market share, they guaranteed the price of heating oil for a decade, but gave customers the right to sell these contracts back to them if prices rose. This was most attractive for a customer.

In order to hedge against such a rise in oil prices, Metallgesellschaft took out Futures contracts. The problem it faced, however, is that Futures contracts were generally run for no more than a year, and so there was a gearing effect for a decade.

Of course, just like the dollar in the Colombo scandal, the Nikkei 225 in the Barings scandal, and interest rates in the Orange County scandal, the price of oil fell rather than rising as expected. Obviously, this led to considerable losses in the Futures market and margin calls.

As time went by, losses just accumulated, finally reaching $1.3 Billion, making this one of the most dramatic failures of a derivative hedging strategy ever recorded.

Summary

There have been a great many other less well known scandals, and probably some which have not been reported. These are problems of concern to anyone with a mortgage or even a pension policy. Most innocent investors will have no idea whether the managers of their mutual funds or their pension funds are taking unsustainable positions based on commodities.

But it is not the derivative instruments themselves that are to blame, any more than motor manufacturers are to blame for road accidents, or fire-arms manufacturers for war. It is the use of these instruments by the individuals and corporations who trade them, which seem to be at fault. The following factors would appear to be common to most scandals.

1.   A period of successful trading, probably just hedging or writing simpler contracts.

2.   A move into more complex areas, with greater gearing and more danger.

3.   Unsupervised individuals taking large positions based on their own judgement and expectations.

4.   Those same individuals, still unsupervised, increasing their positions still further to try to compensate for markets going the wrong way.

5.   Losses coming to light, and trading ceasing for one reason or another.

Chapter Five

Market Analysis

You will not be able to decide on your trading strategy, nor approach the market confidently, unless you have a clear idea of your method of analysis. There are basically two different approaches to this: fundamental analysis and technical analysis. It is not possible to say which is right, or that either is wrong. Nor would it be wise to use only one of the two methods. Clearly, even if you think technical analysis is a complete waste of time, it is, at the very least, a self fulfilling prophecy. Hence, it will have as great, or sometimes a greater bearing on how the markets move than the fundamentals themselves.

Additionally, if you truly believed in technical analysis, then much of the movements which you can predict or chart retrospectively, will have come about as the result of fundamental beliefs.

It would therefore be wise to understand both methods.

Fundamental Analysis

This involves collecting and studying economic data relating to supply and demand in order to forecast likely future price movements. Fundamentalists have to take into account every possible contingency. So, they have to know economics, trends etc. in great depth. In theory, this should be relatively simple. You would start by looking at this year's production, and the overhang from last year. You would then have a fair idea of demands this year and be able to work out how this would affect prices. However, you need to be aware of other factors. For example, one trader may have disproportionate or disguised positions, (see Sumitomo Copper Scandal). Further, there could be some major political development which affects the position. For example, the recent north European BSE epidemic, has had a major effect on the price of beef, with so many herds having to be slaughtered.

Fundamental analysis, therefore, is clearly an important method of giving yourself an edge in producing your forecasts, but you do have to be aware that all bets can be off suddenly as a result of some unforeseen factor.

Technical Analysis

This is perhaps far more interesting to the futures trader. There are a great many critics of technical analysis because of how it works. It seeks to express past price movements as part of a trend, and then simply assume the carrying on of that trend in the future. For example, imagine the price of gold has been increasing at a steady rate over the previous six months. The technical analyst might look at this, draw a line on his chart, and then continue that line showing further growth for the next six months.

At this point, many people want to abandon technical analysis for good. How can the simple drawing of a line on a piece of paper seek to express the change in price of an asset so closely bound up with the intricacies and complexities of the world economy? Of course, it can't. What it can do, however, is make the market aware that this is what a vast number of participants think, they will believe that gold is continuing to rise and will therefore buy it. This means that those who don't believe in technical analysis will also have to buy it, and lo and behold, the price continues to increase.

But, there is rather more to it than this. Imagine, for example, that the trading range of a particular stock or commodity can be expressed between two parallel lines on a graph. At some stage, the line of the price chart may actually break out or pull back from one of the trend lines, either at the top or at the bottom. When this happens, it will be a selling or buying signal for many, even those who do not believe in technical analysis as discussed above.

Perhaps an individual has simply said to himself *"When gold reaches $400 and ounce, I am out"*. But, there could be something much more "fundamental" about it. When gold reaches a certain price, it is a hedge against inflation. Further, when inflation reaches a certain level, gold is still a hedge against inflation!

When the Stock Markets, or other intangibles, start to crash, there is a flight to quality. So, clearly, the whole thing is interrelated. But, nonetheless, the chartists just sit back with their mechanical programmes and carry a disciplined way forward.

The Charts Themselves

There are as many different charts as there are trading systems, but you should be aware of some of the main ones. For example, Figure 5.1 below shows a classic up-trend channel where a price has traded within a particular range, but the range has moved in a generally upward trend.

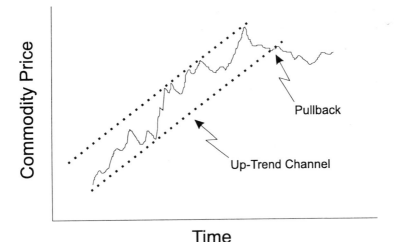

Figure 5.1

Figure 5.2 shows a chart breakout where the commodity price has broken through the long term resistance level, but as the chart progresses, it establishes a second resistance level and a second set of trend lines.

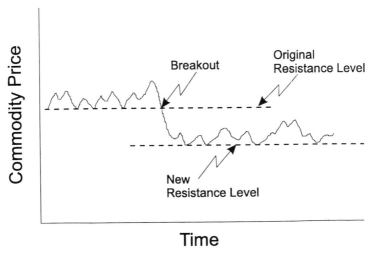

Figure 5.2

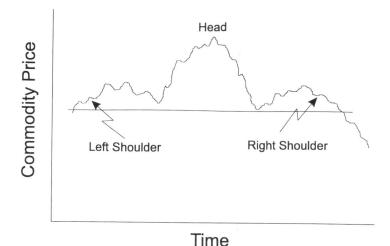

Figure 5.3

Figure 5.3 shows a head and shoulders formation, which is one of the most common reversal trend line indicators. The name, quite clearly, comes from the appearance of the graph itself. If one draws a straight line below the shoulders and head, then when the price movement breaks through this neckline, then the value should drop still further.

Double tops, and their inverts of double bottoms, shown in Figure 5.4, appear something like the head and shoulders without the head. There are even triple tops also known as a 'Total Recall', which are more like a head and shoulders, but with a head the same size as the shoulders.

Another important technical analysis system, which most people will already be aware of is that of moving averages. You can calculate these for any period, be it days, weeks or months. And you can then express them on a chart. Basically, you choose your closing price for a commodity contract over a series of days.

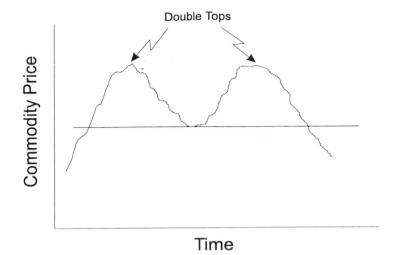

Figure 5.4

What traders often do is use combinations of moving averages. For example, you might have a set of moving averages with different lengths, say a four, nine day and eighteen day moving average. The slowest moving average would give you a long term trend. The movement of this slow moving average in relation to the faster moving average, the four day trend, would give you your buying and selling signals.

It will be a buy-signal when the faster average crosses above the slower, and the sell signal when it crosses below. Your choice of the right types of moving average will be dependant on your activity in the market. Frequent traders, like market traders, may compare hourly averages with daily averages, while fund managers may compare weekly and even monthly averages.

For more details on moving averages, alternative technical indicators like the Momentum indicator, Relative Strength Index, Volume Accumulator Index and oscillators like the MACD

(Moving Average Convergence/Divergence) see *Timing the Financial Markets: Charting Your Way to Profit* or *Understand Financial Risk in a Day* (both published by Take That Ltd. - details on page 95 & 96).

Structural Analysis

Technical analysts often believe in the laws of nature. Accordingly, there are certain technical trends which can be predicted and understood.

For example, seasonal patterns will dictate the prices of commodities such as wheat. And it is possible to prove that peak prices in a particular commodity generally occur between the same period of every year. There are, of course, other cycles which may be shorter or longer than the seasons themselves.

Elliott Waves

Elliott Waves are based on the principle that market behaviour tends to ebb and flow in recognisable patterns, and that these patterns are repeated. Prices are moving in five recognisable waves, following the primary trends. When they move against this trend, they do so in three waves, so that the pattern on a chart is relatively volatile and peaky, rather than a smooth line. If you can figure out exactly where you are in any particular wave, then you should be well placed to benefit from subsequent movements.

Gann Numbers

Many believe that precise mathematical patterns govern everything in the world, but particularly commodity markets.

Mathematics has long fascinated mankind, and the belief is that with odd numbers such as Pi which can be worked out to billions of places without every repeating or coming to a conclusion, or strange calculable relationships between the angles in geometric shapes, that there must also be some order to the apparent chaos of stock and commodity markets. W D Gann claims to have made millions from this type of analysis, and so if you are particularly interested in the details of markets, rather than the conceptual approach, it might well be worth making a further study of his writings. (See Bibliography).

Conclusion

You cannot ignore technical analysis nor can you ignore fundamental analysis. Moreover, it would be wise to be aware of some of the less substantiated theories such as astrological analysis. Superstition can also play its part, just wait for a Stock Market index in the west to reach 666, or in the east when it reaches 88888. The message is clear, you must be aware of all the factors that might affect your approach to the market.

What Would You Do?

On the following page is an interesting position which occurred in the NYMEX Platinum market. The chart uses real data and produces several, often contradictory, indicators. What would you do in this situation? Would you

●   Go long,
●   Go short, or
●   Stay out of the market altogether?

Platinum Commodity Price Chart (Traded on NYMEX)

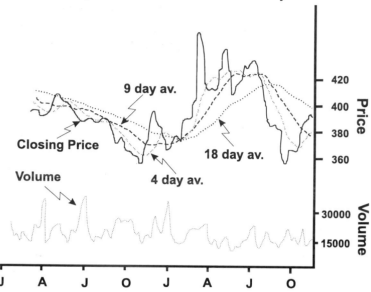

To help you make your decision, here are a few interpretations from the chart plus a few others, such as open interest, which apply to associated data. If you want to test yourself properly, cover these up until you've drawn your own conclusions.

Short Term Interpretation

The market is slightly bullish since the fast moving average is above the slow moving average. You may want to wait for more movement in the same direction to be certain.

Long Term Interpretation

The market is bearish because the fast moving average is below the slow moving average.

Swing Index & Ultimate Oscillator

The swing index has crossed the zero line, identifying it as a short term pivot point and indicating that the market may be about to change direction. The short term Ultimate Oscillator shows no divergence with the market and is neutral - so it does not indicate a change in the market.

MACD

The MACD is in bullish territory since the long term trend is down, but the short term trend is up. This has not, however, generated a buy or sell signal on this chart (when the fast moving average crosses the slow moving average).

Momentum

The momentum is above zero (around 7.0), indicating the market is overbought. The long term analysis of momentum indicates a modest downturn in the market.

Open Interest

The Open Interest is decreasing indicating lower liquidity in the market - expect increased volatility.

RSI

The RSI is at 48.53, indicating 'oversold'. This is not very strong, however, and a stronger signal would be required before going bullish.

(Turn to Page 84 to find out what happened)

Chapter Six

Conclusion

The attractions of trading in commodities are many. Through gearing you can use your capital extremely efficiently. Moreover, whether the markets are rising or falling, you are in a position to make profits. There is a diverse range of underlying commodities which you might use, from the naturally occurring to the abstract index.

There are many different markets through which you might trade, in all major currencies. You can trade on a 24 hour basis, closing out positions daily, or you can take longer term trends. You can buy or sell short term or long term. You can write uncovered positions or ensure you always have stop loss mechanisms in place. You can trade on your own or in concert with others.

You can create a strategy which suits almost any individual and takes into account his or her psychological requirements. You can trade on a simple conceptual basis, or with any degree of detail and analysis you might require. You can fine-tune the risk profile to suit your capital available, and continue to re-tune it as you go.

In short, the world of commodities present you with a flexible, exciting way of taking part in the world's economies. The odds are stacked against you, but the rewards are commensurately large. Be prepared, work hard, and remain disciplined, and you stand as good a chance as the next man. Good Luck!

Appendix A

Computer Systems

I am frequently asked whether or not computer systems are necessary for the creation of successful trading strategies within the market. Of course, if you cannot trade successfully without a computer, you are unlikely to be able to do so with one. But, it is undeniable that even basic spreadsheet programmes will save you an immense amount of time.

You can run various different models much more quickly by using computer techniques, than you can with your pad and pen. Moreover, you can obtain historic data relatively cheaply and study it yourself with your own particular slant on matters.

Where it gets even more interesting, of course, is with bespoke trading programmes. If you are trading privately, you are unlikely to be able to have a software house produce a bespoke programme for you at a sensible cost. However, unless your approach is desperately sophisticated, it should be possible for you to create your own system.

For example, it requires very little computer knowledge to be able to create a graph with trend lines. By constantly inputting prices, as frequently as you like, you will soon be able to see before your very eyes, when a trend line is being broken. Of course, other professional investors will have seen it first, or even anticipated it, but at least you will be ahead of many.

So, use your computer as a means of analysing historical data more rapidly, and running future models to test whether they are likely to work in a variety of different circumstances, for example, should there be shortages or severe oversupply. Once you have made enough money, you might be able to have your own programmes written, and who knows, even sell them to other traders!

Other People's Systems

Of course, there is much to be learned from other people. Perhaps the best example of this is for you to re-read the chapter on Failures again to remind yourself of your own fallibility.

But, when it comes down to the crunch, it is no use listening to friends, other professionals, analysts or whoever, and allowing them to make decisions for you. You will make your own decisions, and you will live with them, right or wrong.

Appendix B

Commodities traded on LIFFE

Robusta Coffee

Coffee is considered to be the foremost agricultural commodity. It comes second only to oil in terms of international trade, and significantly influences the economics of more than 40 producing countries. More than 20 million people are employed in its production.

LIFFE's Robusta Coffee futures contract is the most traded coffee futures contract in the world. Hedgers in this market use it as an integral part of their strategy to minimise potential losses which could occur with unfavourable movements of the coffee price.

The contract is quoted in US dollars, which is the primary currency used in the coffee trade. The quality is assured by stiff control measures supervised by the exchange.

No. 5 White Sugar

A common compliment to coffee, white sugar was once considered to be a luxury item. It is now an important ingredient in the majority of food and beverage products. Around 115 million tonnes of sugar are consumed each year in all of its forms.

London houses a number of firms with considerable experience in all areas of sugar production. So LIFFE is a key sugar futures trading centre, making its No.5 White Sugar contract the most traded in the world.

No.7 Cocoa Futures

This is, perhaps, a surprisingly valuable commodity, which accounts for over $4.5 billion in trade between developed and developing countries. The main producers are countries in West Africa, the Far East and Latin America, some of whom rely almost entirely on the money earned from its export.

The No.7 Cocoa Futures contract was launched on LIFFE in 1928 and is recognised around the world as a benchmark for the physical commodities price; it is quoted in sterling and tonnes. Somewhat unusually, all grades of fermented cocoa are deliverable against the contract with established differentials being due.

BIFFEX Futures

BIFFEX allows ship operators, charterers and owners to protect themselves from the risks of volatility in the shipping rates market. A standardised contract is traded on LIFFE which is settled against an index of international dry bulk 'spot market' voyages, known as the Baltic Freight Index.

A charterer may be concerned that freight shipping rates may rise and eliminate any profit they may have made from trading their physical commodity. To protect against this they may buy a BIFFEX futures contract. If rates do rise, the increase in cost of shipping will be offset by the increase in value of the futures contract. Obviously the ship owner can protect themselves against falling rates by selling BIFFEX futures.

By using BIFFEX it is possible to hedge forward freight shipping rates for up to 18 months forward.

Such an index based futures contract does not give the possibility of 'delivery' in settlement of a position. So any contracts which are left open on the last trading day are settled in cash based on the average of the Baltic Freight Index over the last five days of the settlement month.

Potato Futures

Potato Futures are well known for their volatility. Most of this is down to the time between the harvest in the autumn to the time they are finally used - weather, storage factors and the ratio of imports to exports being a major influence on the price. Expected profit can therefore turn into a big loss if prices go the wrong way.

Wheat Futures

The grain industry is a worldwide multi-billion pound industry which has the need for sophisticated marketing. Every time wheat changes hands in the physical market there is a very large amount of money at stake in various futures centres.

Market expectations are primarily affected by weather conditions in the main producing countries, quality considerations, supply and demand trends, and the ratio of imports to exports.

In addition, currency fluctuations impact on price movement as do the major political decisions taken on wheat issues by the likes of the EEC. Prudent use of the futures market helps protect those in the industry (growers, merchants and compounders) from these risks.

Barley Futures

Almost exactly the same influences as the Wheat futures.

Bibliography

BHATTACHARYA, M - "**Price changes are related to securities in a case of call options and stocks**", The Journal of Financial and Quantitative Analysis 22, Number 1 March 1987.

BERNSTEIN J - "**Facts on Futures. Insights and strategies for winning in the Futures markets**", 1987, Probus Publishing Company.

BERNSTEIN J - "**The Investors Quotient**",1981, John Wiley & Sons.

BERNSTEIN, S - "**Understand Derivatives in a Day**", 1996 & 1998, Take That Ltd.

COX, JOHN & RUBENSTEIN, M - "**Options Markets**", 1985, Prentice Hall.

COX, JOHN, INGERSOL, JONATHAN JNR & ROSS, STEVEN - "**The relation between forward prices and futures prices**", Journal of Financial Economics 9, Number 4. December 1981.

DUNN, D & HARGITT E - "**Point and Figure Commodity Trading in Computer Evaluation**", Dunn & Hargitt.

ELLIOT, R N - "**The Wave Principle**", 1938, Elliott.

ENG, WILLIAM F - "**Options Trading Strategies that Work**", Kogan Page.

FROST, R J - "**Options on Futures - A Hands-on Workbook of Market Proven Strategies**", Probus Publishing.

GANN, WILLIAM D - "**How to Make Profits in Commodities**", 1951, Lambert - Gann.

KAUFFMAN, P J - "**Handbook of Futures Market. Commodity Financial Stock Index and Options**", 1984, John Wiley & Sons.

KIAM, ALEX - "**Understand Financial Risk in a Day**", 1997, Take That Ltd..

KOLB, R W - "**Understand Futures Markets**", 1991, Kolb Publishing.

SCHWAGER, JACK - "**A Complete Guide to Futures Markets**", John Wiley & Sons.

TEWELES, RICHARD J, HARLOW, CHARLES V STONE, H L - "**The Commodity Futures Game, Who Wins, Who Loses. Why?**", 1974, McGraw Hill.

WASENDORF, R R - "**Commodities Trading, The Essential Primer**", 1985, Dow Jones Irwin.

YATES, JIM - "**The Options Strategy Spectrum**", Business One Irwin.

What would you do? (from page 73)

Within a couple of days the price had dropped by more than 20 ticks to 370 and all chart analyses indicated an extremely bearish market.

Glossary

ABANDONED OPTION - This refers to the situation where an option is not exercised nor sold, and is simply left to expire.

ACTUALS - The physical asset underlying a commodity futures contract, rather than the contract itself.

ADJUSTED STRIKE PRICE - Sometimes the strike price of an option needs to be adjusted if there has been a rights issue or some other alteration.

AGGREGATION - A system under which all futures positions, owned or controlled by a particular trader, can be combined in order to comply with reporting limits.

AMERICAN OPTION - This is an option that may be capable of exercise at any time leading up to the expiration date. (In contrast to the European option).

ARBITRAGE - A system whereby advantage is taken of a differential in pricing between similar financial instruments or indexes, sometimes in different markets, or different currencies. The simultaneous purchase of one commodity against the sale of another in an attempt to make a profit from price distortions.

ARBITRAGEUR - A trader who seeks to make a profit from arbitrage.

ARCH - A method of estimating future implied volatility.

AT THE MONEY OPTION - This refers to an option where the strike price is equal to the present market value of the underlying security.

AVERAGING - Sometimes when a price is moving against a trader, he will continue to buy the contract in question as the price falls. This will give him a lower average price, and there-fore a lower exit price at which he can make a profit. By av-eraging down, it might be possible to close out the first con-tracts in the series at a loss, but, overall, make a profit on the book of options. (See Egyptian Ratchet).

BACK SPREAD - This is a position where more long options are written than short options on the same underlying stock. The idea would be to profit from major movements in the un-derlying stock.

BASIS POINT - This is a method of expressing differences in interest rate yields. For example, the difference between 10.05 and 10.10 is 5 basis points. This is particularly important when calculating interest rates swaps.

BASIS RISK - A risk brought about by changes in Spreads.

BED AND BREAKFASTING - This refers to the sale and immediate re-acquisition of a particular investment in order to wash out the capital gain.

BEAR MARKET - This is a depressed market where prices are moving downwards.

BEAR SPREAD - The sale of a Call option, or the purchase of a Put option with a lower or higher strike price, with a simul-taneous purchase of another Call or Put option with higher or lower strike prices.

BETA - A measure of market risk.

BLACK SCHOLES PRICING MODEL - A method used to calculate the theoretical value of an option based on the stock price, the strike price, interest rates, time value, volatility and dividends.

BONUS ISSUE - New Shares issued to existing share-holders increasing the amount they hold, but depressing the price accordingly. This will often result in the need to ad-just an option price.

BOX SPREAD - A four sided option spread involving a long Call and a short Put, with a short Call and a long Put at another strike price. This is often referred to as a synthetic stock position.

BUCKETING - The illegal practice of taking orders to buy or sell without actually executing those orders, and the illegal use of a client's margin deposit without disclosure.

BULL MARKET - A market where prices are generally moving upwards. (See Bear market).

BULL SPREAD - A strategy intended to limit risk and also profit by buying an option and selling another at a higher strike price with the same expiration date. This would allow the trader to profit from any change in price relationship.

BUTTERFLY SPREAD - Another strategy to limit both risk and profit, by, for example, buying one Put at a high strike price, and selling two Puts at a middle strike price, whilst buying one Put at the lowest strike price.

BUY-WRITE - A system whereby the underlying stock is purchased and then a call option written on it. This is covered call option writing and is far safer than going naked.

CARRYING BROKER - A member of a commodity exchange, usually a clearing house member, through whom other brokers can clear all or some of their trades.

CHARTING - The use of graphs and charts in order to produce technical analysis of markets and plot trends of price movements and so on.

CHRISTMAS TREE SPREAD - A process involving six options and four strike prices in an effort to limit risk.

CHURNING - The unethical and repeated sale and purchase of securities within a portfolio with the aim of generating commission rather than in the best interest of the portfolio holder.

CLOSE OUT - If there is an open position, to purchase the necessary contract in order to balance that position so that delivery can be made.

COMMISSIONS - The amounts charged by brokers on sale and purchase transactions from which they make their living.

COMMODITY POOL - A way in which funds from a number of different people are grouped together in order to trade futures contracts.

CONDOR SPREAD - A process to limit risk by purchasing four options at four strike prices. A long call spread would involve buying one Call at the lowest strike, selling one at the second strike, selling a further one at the third strike and buying one again at the fourth strike.

CONTRACT - A term of reference describing a unit of trading of a commodity.

CONVERTIBLE STOCK - A share which carries a set dividend but has the right to convert to ordinary equity at a set date in the future.

CO-VARIANTS - A measure statistically of how to variables act together.

COVER - To offset an existing futures transaction with an equal opposite transaction.

COVERED CALL OPTION - A Call option where the writer owns the individual stock on which the option is based. He can therefore make delivery if exercised.

COVERED PUT OPTION - A Put option where the writer has not gone naked, either by shorting the stock or having sufficient cash to cover the exercise.

CYCLE - Different series of options have different expiration dates. These are referred to as the Cycles.

DAY TRADING - The practice of taking positions in commodities which must be liquidated at the end of each day.

DECAY - The value of an option will decline with time, notwithstanding other influences on its pricing. This is know as decay, to time delay.

DEFAULT - The failure to meet the obligations of a futures contract.

DEFERRED DELIVERY - The distant delivery months in which futures trading takes place, rather than the nearby futures delivery month.

DELTA - This refers to the amount by which the price of an option can change based on a similar change in the underlying instrument. For example, an option with a Delta of 0.5 will move 0.5 units in price for every one unit movement in the underlying stock.

DIAGONAL SPREAD - This is a strategy where two options of the same type, but with different strike prices and expiration dates are bought simultaneously.

DISCRETIONARY ACCOUNT - Where an investor gives a professional discretion to deal on his behalf.

EFFICIENT FRONTIER - A set of portfolios where risk and reward are optimised.

ELASTICITY - A means of expressing the fact that price changes can create or increase the demand for a particular commodity. Inelasticity would be when man demand for a commodity exists largely irrespective of the price.

EXERCISE PRICE - This is the price in an option contract where the buyer of the option may purchase or sell the relevant commodity during the life of the contract.

FIBONACCI NUMBER - A sequence of numbers (0,1,2,3,5,8,13,21,34 etc.) discovered by the Italian mathematician Leonardo de Pise in the 13th Century. It is the basis of the Elliott Wave theory and works by the successive number being the sum of the previous two.

FLOOR TRADERS - Members of an Exchange who actually trade on the floor of the Exchange.

FORWARD CONTRACTS - A contract where the seller undertakes to deliver a specific financial instrument to a buyer at a date in the future.

FUNDAMENTAL ANALYSIS - An approach to an analysis of markets seeking to predict future movements as a result of underlying fundamental factors.

FUTURES CONTRACTS - A contract to buy or to sell a specified quantity of a particular commodity or instrument at a named date in the future.

GAMMA - The rate at which a delta of a stock changes in relation to the asset price. A second order measure of the exposure of an option to the underlying prize.

HEDGE - To cover a particular position or exposure by using a derivative instrument or some other strategy.

HEDGING - The use of options and futures in order to safeguard against a decline or increase in the price of a particular commodity which the hedger either owns or knows he must buy.

INDEX OPTION - An option on a particular index such as the FTSE.

IN THE MONEY OPTION - The option which has an immediate value, for example, where the strike price of a Call is below the current market price.

IRON BUTTERFLY - The trading strategy with limited risk that involves a long or short straddle and a short or long strangle.

LIMIT ORDER - A transaction in which the client sets a limit as to the price or the time of dealing, or both. This contrasts with the Market Order, which should be dealt with immediately.

LIQUIDITY RISK - The risk associated with the inability to raise cash.

LONG HETCH - A process of buying futures contracts to protect against possible increased prices of commodities.

MARGIN - A payment deposited by a client dealing in derivatives. The money is placed with a broker or a clearing house to ensure against losses on open contracts.

MARGIN CALL - A request from the clearing house or broker that the options trader increases the amount of deposit.

MODEL - A word used to explain such things such as the Black Scholes, the Tarantula or the Butterfly.

NAKED WRITING - A process whereby options contracts are effected without possession of the underlying stock.

OFFSET - Liquidating the purchase of futures through the sale of an equal number of contracts with the same delivery month. Alternatively, covering a short sale of futures contracts via the purchase of an equal number of contracts for the same delivery month.

OPEN OUT CRY - A method of making bids in the pits of commodity exchanges.

OPEN POSITION - A trading position which has not yet been exercised or closed.

OPTION PREMIUM - The money which the buyer pays to the writer of the option for granting the option.

OUT OF THE MONEY OPTIONS - This refers to a situation where the exercise price is greater than the market price of the underlying stock, or, if a Put option, less than the market price. A Call option with a strike price higher or a Put option with a strike price lower than the current market value of the assets in question.

OVER-BOUGHT - The view that the market price has risen too steeply in respect of underlying factors.

OVER-SOLD - The view that the market price has declined too   steeply in respect of underlying factors.

OVER-BOUGHT / OVER-SOLD - A broker or analyst may consider the market to be over-bought, i.e. that prices have risen too quickly when judged against the fundamentals.

POSITION - A commitment to the market based on contracts bought or sold.

PREMIUM - The amount paid for an option or taken as a result of writing an option.

PROFIT TAKING - At a particular point in the market, traders may reach selling triggers and they will take profits. Market falls due to profit taking are generally less serious than those due to a fundamental change in sentiment.

RALLY - An upward movement of prices.

RATCHET - A means of averaging through successive purchases (see Egyptian Ratchet).

R H O - A measure of the exposure of an option to interest rates.

RIGHTS ISSUE - A company often wishes to raise capital and therefore issues further shares, but always to existing investors first in the ratio of their existing holdings.

THE SFA (SEC) - The Security and Futures Association which regulates stockbroking activities, and in the United States, the Securities and Exchange Commission which carries out the same role.

SHORT - An individual who has sold stock that he does not hold is said to be short of that stock. A trader who has sold a commodity or a commodity contract which he does not have, intending to close out the transaction before the delivery date.

SHORT HEDGE - Selling futures to protect against possible falling prices in commodities.

SPECULATOR - Someone whose aim is to benefit from price changes and profit through the sale of purchase of commodity futures contracts.

SPOT - The price given for immediate delivery.

STOCHASTIC - Something which evolves randomly over time.

STOP LOSS - A risk management technique used to close out a losing position at a given point.

STRADDLE - A strategy whereby a long Put and a long Call option on the same underlying stock are written, with the same exercise price on the same expiration date.

STRANGLE - A strategy whereby a long Put and a long Call option are written on the same underlying stock with same expiration dates but different exercise prices.

SUPPORT - A price level for a falling market at which it has stopped falling.

TARANTULA - A trading model developed for use in options and futures markets (see also Spider's Web).

TECHNICAL ANALYSIS - An approach to analysis of futures markets and anticipated future trends of commodity prices.

TIME VALUE - With an option, the value may decrease over time. The time value is an important component in pricing options.

TREND LINE - A line that connects either a series of highs or lows in a trend. This can either be a support level, or a resistance level, depending on whether trends are on the up or on the down.

UNCOVERED OPTIONS - The writing of options without possessing the underlying stock.

VERTICAL SPREADS - Buying and selling Puts or Calls with the same expiration date but different strike prices.

VOLATILITY - The actual, or expected fluctuation in price of an share or option.

WASTING ASSET - All option contracts are wasting assets in that their value declines with time. This may be compared with a lease on a house or flat whereby, as time goes on, the value of that lease reduces, all other things being equal.

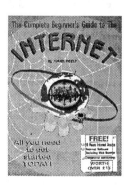

The Complete Beginner's Guide to The Internet   £4.95

Everywhere you turn these days, it's Internet this, Cyberspace that and Superhighway the other. Indeed, hardly a day goes by without us being bombarded with information and reasons why you should be on the Net. But none of that is of much help in making an informed decision about joining and using the Internet.

What exactly is The Internet? Where did it come from and where is it going? And, more importantly, how can everybody take their place in this new community?

The Complete Beginner's Guide to The Internet answers all of those questions and more. On top of being an indispensable guide to the basics of Cyberspace, it is the lowest priced introduction on the market by a long way at a *surfer-friendly £4.95* (alternative books cost around £30).

Understand
Derivatives
in a Day

By understanding how derivatives affect apparently safe investments, such as pensions, endowment mortgages and equity plans, you can make sure your own cash is in good hands.

£6.95

Learn...❑How private investors get started... ❑To Hedge, Straddle and control Risk... ❑Ways to limit the downside but *not* the upside... ❑About *risk free* derivative strategies... ❑Trading Psychology - Fear, Hope and Greed... ❑Also, the History of Derivatives; Currency Speculation; Long and Short puts; Tarantula Trading; and much more.

Create Your Own Web Site

The World Wide Web is being transformed into an important business and communications tool. Millions of computer users around the globe now rely on the Web as a prime source of information and entertainment.

Once you begin to explore the wonders of the Internet, it isn't long before the first pangs of desire hit – you want your own Web site.

Whether it is to showcase your business and its products, or a compilation of information about your favourite hobby or sport, creating your

£5.95

own Web site is very exciting indeed. But unless you're familiar with graphics programs and HTML (the "native language" of the Web), as well as how to upload files to the Internet, creating your Web page can also be very frustrating!

But it doesn't have to be that way. This book, written by an Internet consultant and graphics design specialist, will help demystify the process of creating and publishing a Web site.

Understand
Financial Risk
in a Day

Risk management is all about minimising risks and maximising opportunities. Those who understand what they should be doing, as a result of their risk calculations, will usually come out as winners. Those who flail around in the dark will, more often than not, be the losers.

Understand Financial Risk in a Day is a perfect introduction to the subject. Light on detailed formulae and heavy on easy-to-follow examples it will lead the reader to a

£6.95

greater awareness of how to evaluate the risks they are facing and adapt a strategy to create the best possible outcome. All of the latest risk management techniques are discussed and the best tools selected for dealing with each aspect.

Timing The Financial Markets: Charting Your Way to Profit

Timing The Financial Markets shows all levels of investors, step-by-step, how to construct charts and graphs of price movements for bonds, shares and commodities. Then it explains, in easy-to-understand language, how to interpret the results and turn them into profit.

£6.95